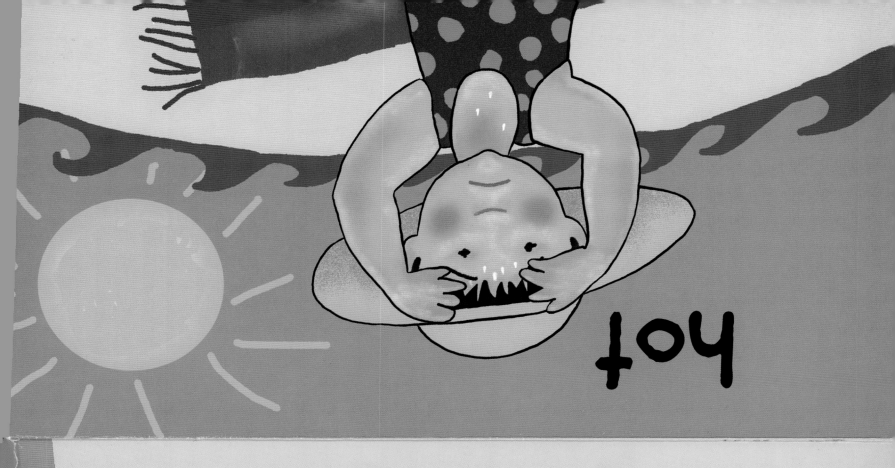

toy

DOUBLE DELIGHT

Opposites

Mary Novick & Sybel Harlin

BACKPACK**BOOKS**

○

NEW YORK

cold

dn

small

down

big

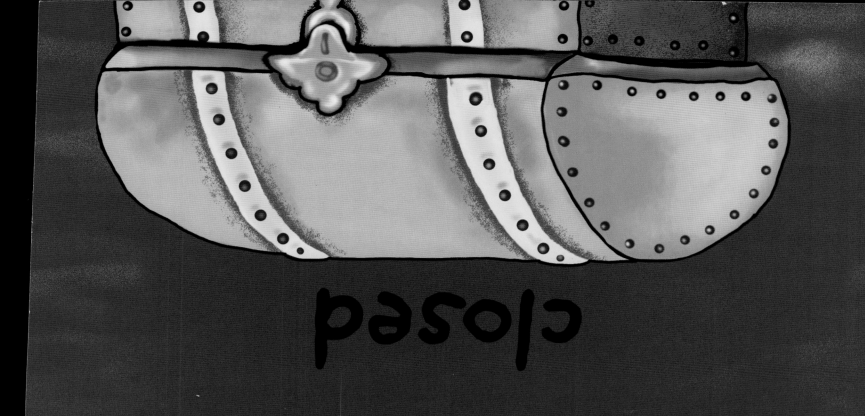

closed

clean

open

heavy

happy

light

pos

back

over

night

short

day

long

awake

below

asleep

above

slow

Backpack Books
122 Fifth Avenue
New York, NY 10011

ISBN 0-7607-6490-5

Printed and bound in Thailand

05 06 07 08 09 MCH 10 9 8 7 6 5 4 3 2 1

Illustrated, designed, and typeset by Jenny Hale.

Library of Congress Cataloging-in-Publication Data available upon request.

First published in 2001 by Little Hare Books
4/21 Mary Street Surry Hills
NSW 2010
Australia